BLACK MEXICAN

Rachel Lynett

BROADWAY PLAY PUBLISHING INC
New York
www.broadwayplaypublishing.com
info@broadwayplaypublishing.com

First edition: December 2023
I S B N: 979-8-88856-004-4

Book design: Marie Donovan
Page make-up: Adobe InDesign
Typeface: Palatino

NOTE

Reference: https://www.theroot.com/a-white-woman-admits-shes-been-rachel-dolezal-ing-us.

I let it go after Rachel Dolezal. I will not let it go after Jessica Krug.

The thing that upset me the most about Krug was that she tried on many different Caribbean identities as if there's no nuance. As if people who are actually from the Caribbean aren't fighting to be recognized as part of Latinidad.

"To an escalating degree over my adult life, I have eschewed my lived experience as a white Jewish child in suburban Kansas City under various assumed identities within a Blackness that I had no right to claim: first North African Blackness, then US rooted Blackness, then Caribbean rooted Bronx Blackness. I have not only claimed these identities as my own when I had absolutely no right to do so—when doing so is the very epitome of violence, of thievery and appropriation, of the myriad ways in which non-Black people continue to use and abuse Black identities and cultures—but I have formed intimate relationships with loving, compassionate people who have trusted and cared for me when I have deserved neither trust nor caring."—Jessica Krug

This pissed me off. So I decided to write a play about it.

CHARACTERS & SETTING

five women:

ZOE, *mid 30s, Afro-Latina/e, Dominican-Haitian artist*

XIMENA/LOREN, *early 40s, "Cuban", professor, specializes in art across the Latin American diaspora in the contemporary era, ZOE's wife*

VALERY, *mid 20s Latina/e, Cuban, graduate student studying Latin American Theatre with a specific focus in set design*

RAFA, *early 30s, Afro-Latina/e, professor at the same university as XIMENA, specializes in Latin American theatre across the diaspora, ZOE's sister, Dominican-Haitian*

ALIA, *late 20s, Black, Belizean, ZOE's assistant and graduate student at the university studying sculpture, artist*

This play takes place in a city that thinks it's super liberal. 2020.

PRODUCTION NOTES

Moment v shift

I have a hard time with the word "beat". For me, moment is a break in the dialogue, a chance for the characters to reassess. Shift is just a sharp turn in dialogue or action. It's not necessarily a pause. A moment is a passive action/pause whereas a shift is an active one.

PLAYWRIGHT'S NOTE ON LATINE/X/A

There are many ways in which we identify and I understand each of us have a different comfort level with Latine, Latinx, Latina… For the purposes of this play, whenever Latine or Latinx and any other variant is written, it's up to the actor and their comfort level which word they'd prefer to use. As there is no reason any of the character cannot be played by transwomen actors, I want to keep the endings/suffixes and pronouns open to interpretation.

NOTE ON MUSIC

For performance of copyrighted songs, arrangements or recordings referenced in this play, permission of the copyright owner(s) must be obtained. Other songs, arrangements or recordings may be substituted provided permission from the copyright owner(s) of such songs, arrangements or recordings is obtained, or songs, arrangements or recordings in the public domain may be substituted.

Scene 1

(In an office, RAFA is working on research and grading papers. She is hyper focused. After a moment or two, VALERY knocks. RAFA looks up and immediately reaches for her mask and puts it on.)

RAFA: Hi. Sorry. I wasn't expecting anyone to stop by.

VALERY: No, it's okay. I'll just I'll keep my distance.

(A moment)

RAFA: Did you have a question about your—

VALERY: My paper got accepted into the conference I was going for.

RAFA: Oh. Congrats!

VALERY: Thanks. I um
I asked Professor Campos to be co-author because I thought it would be more—

RAFA: Valery, we've talked about this. I know I'm your normally your advisor and mentor but you'll need other collaborators and paper about scenic design's intersection with contemporary art in Latin America is more of Dr Campos's field of—

VALERY: Are you close to Professor Campos?

RAFA: Valery is something wrong?

VALERY: No I just
Do you know her well?

RAFA: I know her work very well. She's a leading scholar—

VALERY: I'm not sure who talk to about this but there are only three faculty of color in the entire division so I—

RAFA: If something happened, you should tell me. Now. I don't care who it is or how important they think their work is, if they crossed a line with a student, I will always believe the student and this is not something you should keep to—

VALERY: What? Oh no. It's nothing like that. If anything Professor Campos is too distant.

RAFA: She can be a bit standoff-ish. But putting Dr. Ximena Campos on a paper is—

VALERY: I don't think she's Cuban.

RAFA: What?

VALERY: I don't think
I have a feeling and I can't shake it but I don't think she's Cuban.

RAFA: I know she's light but white Latinos are—

VALERY: I don't think she's Latine at all.

RAFA: Valery, I'm not sure I want to

VALERY: And I think I can prove it but I need help. You say, you've always said you stand by the students. Is that true?

RAFA: Valery, I can't support you—

VALERY: So it's not?

RAFA: This is absurd. She's Cuban.

VALERY: You've met her parents?

RAFA: Of course I
I told you. She's married to my sister so

VALERY: And her parents are Cuban? They said they were Cuban?

RAFA: Valery, I realize Ximena—Dr Campos can be difficult to work with. She's obsessive and specific and can be really demanding. But I'm not sure what you're trying to achieve by—

VALERY: I'm not trying to achieve anything. I just don't like when someone tries on my culture for fun.

RAFA: Valery, what's this really about?

VALERY: I'm Cuban. I know Cubans. Ximena Campos is not Cuban. So if she's lying about being Cuban, what else is she lying about?

RAFA: Valery, I've entertained this long enough. If you want to move forward with this, contact Dean Vilas. I have a lot of work to do.

(VALERY *hesistates for a second before she leaves.*)

Scene 2

(*In her studio,* ZOE *is staring at a blank canvas.* ALIA, *wearing a mask, walks in holding two coffees.*)

ALIA: (*Joking*) So how's the commission coming?

ZOE: Super well. Look, I'm almost finished.

(ALIA *looks at the blank canvas and hands one of the coffees to* ZOE. ALIA *takes off her mask.*)

ALIA: What's this one again?

ZOE: I have to paint a new future for a 2020 world.

ALIA: That's disturbing.

ZOE: It's 20k. I couldn't turn it down. Not after all the work I lost this year.

ALIA: It's a collage of canvases right?

ZOE: Maybe? I don't know. I had this really cool idea to create a bunch of alternate 2020s super imposed onto each other, you know? So it would be this one chaotic cohesive thing. Each different part would be
Ugh, I'm not explaining it well.

ALIA: No, I get it. It sounds cool.

ZOE: How's your work coming along? Didn't you have your art show recently at the university?

ALIA: Well, I thought I had something really smart. And the gallery opening went well…until

ZOE: Oh no what happened? *(Moment)* Alia, what happened?

ALIA: Dr. Campos stopped by.

ZOE: Oh?

ALIA: And called my work appropriative.

ZOE: I'm sorry. She can be a bit, um, I don't know. Overly herself.

ALIA: Yeah. Anyway, it was a mostly good night. Except you know, being told that though the African diaspora has a greater reach than most know but even Black people must be conscious of when—

ZOE: Ugh I know the spiel and I hate it. She's been in a mood. She shouldn't have been an ass.

ALIA: They pulled my work from consideration for the award.

ZOE: What?!

ALIA: Yeah. It's 2020, you know. They felt that I shouldn't have been in the show.

ZOE: That's absurd!

ALIA: I'm Black. And I don't usually talk about my—
ZOE: You're Belizean!

ALIA: Yeah but a lot of people don't—

ZOE: That's literally in Central America.

ALIA: It's not considered a "Latino" country.

ZOE: It's in Central America! You speak Spanish!

ALIA: Speaking Spanish isn't exactly
It's fine. I'm not upset about it anymore. I don't want to
take up a space I shouldn't have.

ZOE: It is not fine. Am I suddenly not Latine enough
because I'm Haitian?

ALIA: You're also Dominican.

ZOE: It's the same goddamn island. Oh my God. This is
No. I'm going to talk to Ximena, She's gone too far.

ALIA: Please don't talk to her. I don't want to make a
big deal out of it. I was just
I mostly wanted to talk to you about the Afro-Latine
identity and the cross cultures I didn't want

ZOE: Alia, you created an amazing piece of art that
reflects Latinidad in a beautiful and important way.
And I'm not going to let my wife cunt this up for you.

ALIA: Zoe, I really don't want to cause a fight.

ZOE: You know how much I love fighting. It'll be fun.
Now tell me the names of jurors who pulled your work
so I can yell at them too.

(ZOE *goes to get a piece of paper.* ALIA *stares at the blank
canvas.*)

Scene 3

(*Later that day,* ZOE, *wearing headphones, is still in her
studio. The canvas is making some progress and has art on it
but it isn't good.*)

(RAFA *enters and looks around at the art work. She's proud of her big sister.* ZOE *notices her.*)

ZOE: Ay, you're trying to give me a heart attack.

RAFA: I brought dinner.

(ZOE *walks over to* RAFA. RAFA *hands her the brown paper bag.* ZOE *inspects it.*)

RAFA: Meat pies from the Jamaican place on 8th.

ZOE: Was Benny there?

RAFA: …Yes.

ZOE: When are you finally going to let that man take you out?

RAFA: When I'm ready to be taken out.

ZOE: You've been single for two years.

RAFA: You sound like mom.

ZOE: Well, what're you waiting for?

RAFA: The desire to want to have another person around me.

ZOE: Nobody said around you. We're talking about in you.

(RAFA *playfully throws something at* ZOE. ZOE *starts to eat the meat pies.*)

ZOE: Okay, why are you really here?

RAFA: I can't visit my sister.

ZOE: You don't usually come to my studio.

RAFA: I tried your house. Ximena said you were here.

ZOE: Oh! That reminds me. (*She pulls out her phone.*) I need to send an angry text message.

RAFA: What?

ZOE: I like to send vague, angry text messages to Ximena so she can brace herself for when I'm coming home mad.

RAFA: And you and mom wonder why I want to be single.

(ZOE *finishes her text message.*)

ZOE: What's up?

RAFA: I need to ask you something.

ZOE: Oh. This never ends well.

RAFA: It's something kind of crazy.

ZOE: I'm not doing anymore of your weird plays, Rafa. I told you I'm not an actor and no offense but you're a scholar, not—

RAFA: No, it's not that.

A student came to me today and said she doesn't think Ximena is Cuban.

ZOE: Well that's ridiculous.

RAFA: Yeah. I know

And I mentioned that there was white Latinos but

ZOE: But what?

RAFA: I feel crazy but I

So I asked my student to leave and I dismissed it. But then I
Her parents weren't at the wedding.

ZOE: Rafa, what is this?

RAFA: I just
Have you met her parents?

ZOE: You mean her racist, homophobic parents who didn't like my complexion because no puede mejorar la raza con una negra.

RAFA: I know this is…a hard subject. And I'm not trying to I'm just asking, Zoe.
You know I wouldn't be bringing this up if it didn't deeply bother me.

ZOE: Why is everyone suddenly playing gatekeeper with Latinidad today? The reason I'm yelling at Ximena is because she said that Alia shouldn't have submitted to the Latin Art Show.

RAFA: Alia isn't Latinx. She's Black.

ZOE: Not you too, Rafa.

RAFA: She's always only said she was Black.

ZOE: No, she's said she's Belizean and you assumed And also mom says she's Black too. When enough people tell you you're not something, you start to believe them.

RAFA: Mom is different.

ZOE: No, she isn't.

RAFA: Mom has Taíno blood.

ZOE: Rafa. Are you kidding? Taíno blood? Mom still calls herself Black.

RAFA: She speaks Spanish.

ZOE: So does Alia.

(*Moment*)

RAFA: Have you met Ximena's parents? Or gone to Cuba to meet her family there?

ZOE: No. Of course not. Why would I
I don't have the energy for whatever this is. I need to finish working so I can go home. To my Cuban wife.

RAFA: I don't mean to—

ZOE: Ya, Rafa. I'm tired. And not even half-way done.

RAFA: Yeah, okay. Sorry.

(RAFA leaves. ZOE angrily eats the meat pies.)

Scene 4

(The next morning. At ZOE and XIMENA's home. ZOE, in her pajamas, is drinking coffee and reading a newspaper. XIMENA comes in, professionally dressed.)

XIMENA: Good morning mi amor.

(XIMENA goes to kiss ZOE but ZOE moves away.)

XIMENA: You're still upset?

ZOE: Yes, I'm still upset.

XIMENA: I didn't realize Alia was Belizean.

ZOE: It's not your place to gatekeep.

XIMENA: You are correct. I am so sorry. How can I fix this?

ZOE: By apologizing.

XIMENA: Great. Done. I will do that.

ZOE: Tonight.

XIMENA: I will text her right now.

ZOE: No, at dinner.

XIMENA: I'm meeting with a student tonight.

ZOE: Invite her to dinner too. We'll all talk about the diaspora and how we all need to be better.

XIMENA: It is unprofessional to invite a student to my home for—

ZOE: We'll sit outside and at a distance. Or cancel your meeting with your student.

XIMENA: It's for a conference. Querida, I'm sorry. I will text Alia and—

ZOE: You will tell Alia to her face that you are sorry and I don't care if your student is there or not.

(*Moment*)

XIMENA: Fine. What time?

ZOE: Seven PM.

XIMENA: May I kiss my wife now?

ZOE: You may.

(XIMENA *kisses* ZOE.)

XIMENA: I have so much work to do and all I want to do is stay home and get back in bed and show you just how sorry I am.

ZOE: Meh. I have to paint today. The clock is ticking very loudly.

XIMENA: Switch clocks.

ZOE: (*Sarcastic*) Ha ha ha ha.

(*Shift*)

XIMENA: You are the only person I know who still reads the newspaper in print. Use your phone.

ZOE: I hate my phone. I wish I could be one of those people who just said "I don't have a phone."

XIMENA: Then be one of those people.

ZOE: (*Ay*) Dio, my mom would move in if she didn't have a way to call me every five minutes.

XIMENA: How is Helene?

ZOE: Crazy. She started a garden.

XIMENA: Oh that's nice. It'll be good—

ZOE: At the park. So she's fighting with the city right now because she says land belongs to God and not us and how dare the city tell her she can't plant tomatoes in earth. La tierra no pertenece a la ciudad. La tierra pertenece a la gente.

XIMENA: Pueblo.

ZOE: What?

XIMENA: Shouldn't it be pueblo?

ZOE: My mom said gente. You know she speaks her own Spanish.

XIMENA: When does she go before city council?

ZOE: I don't know.

You promise not to skip tonight?

XIMENA: I promise.

ZOE: You won't cancel last minute?

XIMENA: I will be there. I will see if the student is comfortable coming over. But I will be here.

ZOE: I'll ask Rafa to come too.

XIMENA: Zoe

ZOE: It's still less than ten people. Just the four of us. Five if your student comes.

(XIMENA *checks the time.*)

XIMENA: I have to go. I love you.

(XIMENA *kisses* ZOE *goodbye.*)

ZOE: Seven PM, Ximena!

XIMENA: Ya te prometo. I'll be there.

(XIMENA *leaves.* ZOE *gets up and mindlessly looks through some things in the kitchen. She sees a photograph and pulls it out. And studies it. Then she makes a face. She sets the photograph down. And leaves. A second before she comes back in, grabs the photograph, and then grabs her coat.*)

Scene 5

(RAFA *is in her office, eating fruit and drinking coffee. She's working. Well, she's trying to work. She's not getting much done.*)

(ZOE, wearing a mask, still in her pajamas, enters the office.

RAFA: Zoe, are you
Are you in your pajamas?

ZOE: I was thinking.

RAFA: Okay. Think quickly. I teach in like 30 minutes.

ZOE: So I was looking through the drawers in the kitchen, you know, standard procrastination stuff. And I found this old picture of mom and dad.

RAFA: Okay.

ZOE: Look at dad. (*She pulls out the picture.*)

RAFA: I'm not sure what the point of this

ZOE: Imagine if someone said "Raul isn't Latino. He's Black. And I'm going to prove it." Wouldn't that infuriate you? I hate that we're all so…I don't know…shitty about how we exclude people across the diaspora.

(VALERY *enters without even of them noticing.*)

RAFA: Zoe, I'm sorry I brought it up but I really need to finish—

VALERY: I have proof! Oh, hi.

RAFA: Valery, this is a really bad time.

VALERY: You asked me to find proof. I found it.

ZOE: I should go. I'm honestly just grumpy and wanted to yell at someone. Bye Rafa. (*She starts to leave.*)

VALERY: I found a picture of Professor—Dr Campos when she was young.

(ZOE *turns around.*)

ZOE: What?!

RAFA: Zoe, you should go.

ZOE: Let me see it. (*She takes the picture.*) This isn't
Ximena. Ximena doesn't This person is blonde.

VALERY: Professor Castillo, who is
Who is this?

RAFA: This is a bad time, Valery.

ZOE: Rafa, you asked for proof?
Are you the student who's been accusing my wife of
(*She looks at the picture again and sits down.*)
This is impossible.

VALERY: Wife?

ZOE: How did you find this?

VALERY: I talked to her brother. He was really hard to
find at first because I didn't
Listen, it's 2020. I can't risk having my career being
launched by a fraud. I needed to know
I'm sorry. I realize this is different for you but—

RAFA: How did you find out she had a brother?

VALERY: So she doesn't have a Facebook. Or any social
media. But she said she went to Mount Holyoke. So I
searched alumni pages there. And that's when I found
Loren Davis. Which, okay, people change their names
all the time for totally valid reasons but—

ZOE: This can't be This isn't
This is ridiculous. There's no way

VALERY: Professor Castillo, we have to do something.
We can't let her continue to pretend like

RAFA: Valery. I shouldn't have asked you to look
further into it. I should've just Can you give us a
minute?

Valery: Um, sure.

(Valery *tries to take the picture back from* Zoe. Zoe *shakes her head.*)

Zoe: What's her brother's name?

Valery: Jimmy. James. But he goes by Jimmy. He's all over social media.

Zoe: I'm assuming you have other copies of this?

Valery: No but I have other proof. I get that this is hard for you but we have to exp ose her. What's she been doing—

Rafa: Give us a minute.

(Valery *leaves.* Zoe *stares at the picture.*)

Zoe: I don't even
I feel like I'm still asleep. This is too fucking surreal.

Rafa: Zoe. We don't know the whole story yet. You can't—

Zoe: Loren Davis. Blonde Loren Davis. My wife has curly black hair and speaks Spanish with a slight Cuban accent. Loren Davis has straight blonde hair and I'm guessing a Midwestern accent?

Rafa: Zoe, do you really want to do this?

Zoe: You were going to do it anyway, right? You asked her to find proof?

Rafa: I didn't
I emailed her and said her claims were inflammatory and if she couldn't prove it, she needed to write a formal apology letter to Doctor—to Ximena.

Zoe: On our wedding certificate, it says Ximena Campos. I've only ever known Ximena Campos.

Rafa: You're accepting something is true without really knowing for sure. Take some time to relax, some

time to just breathe. What is it that mom's always says?
You can't predict the puzzle with just a corner piece.

ZOE: I'm going to head my studio.

RAFA: Zoe, it's a huge misunderstanding. I'm sure of it.
Please don't panic about this.

ZOE: Yeah. I um
Yeah. I should go.

(ZOE *leaves, keeping the picture with her.*)

Scene 6

(XIMENA *sits in her office grading papers. She has her mask
hanging by the side of her ear, just in case. There's a picture
of* ZOE *on her desk. After a beat or two, she notices* ALIA
walk by.)

XIMENA: Alia, do you have a moment?

(*Though we can't see* ALIA *yet, it should be clear that she
hesitates. A beat before she enters, staying by the door.*)

ALIA: Good afternoon, Professor Campos.

XIMENA: I had an interesting talk with Zoe last night.

(ALIA *nods. Says nothing. Wants to leave*)

XIMENA: I know professors can be intimidating
but students should be comfortable voicing their
complaints to us directly.

ALIA: Yeah. I will. Next time.

(*A moment*)

XIMENA: Have you ever been to Belize?

ALIA: Excuse me?

XIMENA: Have you ever been? It's funny. My Cuban
family, the family that's still in Cuba say that I'm not

really Cuban. I'm American because I wasn't born in Cuba.

ALIA: Oh right.

XIMENA: So have you been?

ALIA: Uh yeah. I used to go with my mom in the summer.

XIMENA: Oh that's nice.

ALIA: Yeah. Well, again sorry that I didn't—

XIMENA: And did you speak Spanish there?

ALIA: I don't under—

XIMENA: In Belize. Did you speak Spanish?

ALIA: Dr Campos, is there something else you're trying to ask me?

XIMENA: You don't have to be so formal, Alia. You're my wife's assistant. You've probably been in my home more often than I have. It's just Ximena.

(*Moment*)

ALIA: I guess I don't understand the sudden curiosity about Belize.

XIMENA: I am trying to recognize my blind spots and acknowledge them. I always skpped over Belize in my research because that I thought
Do you know Natasha Mejia?

ALIA: Not well.

XIMENA: She's Belizean and she just considers herself Black. I'm trying to understand the nuance.

(*Moment*)

ALIA: I've already pulled out of the—

XIMENA: I know. I'd like you to resubmit. I was rash and didn't have all the information. I'm sorry.

ALIA: Um, yeah. Thanks. I'll just—

XIMENA: But I want you to take your time and really think through what drives us to occupy certain spaces and what spaces we should remove ourselves from.

ALIA: Yeah. Got it. *(She starts to leave.)*

XIMENA: One last thing.

(XIMENA *pulls out a paper from the file and hands it to* ALIA.*)*

XIMENA: I noticed the Spanish you used in this paper is a sort of Mexican slang. While I'll allow students from Latine/x countries to write in the dialect they're most comfortable, I ask students who are not to write in Spanish, properly.

ALIA: Latinx countries? Don't you mean—

XIMENA: I don't mean to be harsh but as an educator it's my job to teach you what's right and what's wrong. Please make the necessary edits to the Spanish dialect. From Spain. I realize it's a bit of an inconvenience so I'm happy to give you extra time. Let's say you'll get back it to me in a week?

(ALIA *looks at the piece of paper.)*

ALIA: You realize I do speak Spanish right?

XIMENA: I've actually never heard you speak Spanish. I've heard you respond to it but you always answer in English. Perhaps next time we meet, we can talk in Spanish?

(ALIA *says nothing, takes the piece of paper, and leaves the office.)*

Scene 7

(ZOE, *with headphones on, is in her studio, painting furiously. She's not necessarily being productive but the art looks better.*)

(ALIA *approaches with a notebook and some files.*)

ALIA: (*Not seeing the headphones*) So I printed up the contract from MASS MOCA and they changed the terms of the residency so I thought you might want to check that out. Oh! And turns out I can resubmit my—

(ZOE *turns around and jumps. She takes her headphones out.*)

ALIA: Oh sorry. I didn't see your headphones.

ZOE: Oh. It's okay.

ALIA: Um so the contract says they want—

ZOE: Why don't you say you're Afro-Latine?

ALIA: Today has a theme apparently.

ZOE: You identify as Black, right? But both of your parents were born in Belize.

ALIA: We've talked about this before and I really don't want to Zoe, are you okay?

ZOE: I'm curious.

ALIA: It's been a long
Both of my parents aren't Belizean. My dad's, well, my dad's parents were born in Mexico and are Afro-Mexican but he was adopted by a black family so he didn't really It's all really complicated.

ZOE: And your dad's last name is Smith?

ALIA: Rivas but I use my mom's last name. My dad took my mom's Zoe are you sure you're
And even if my dad's last name was Smith, it's not that uncommon. Kiara Smith is Panamanian.

Zoe: Alia, why hadn't you told me about *(your dad)*. You're literally Afro-Latine.

Alia: I never said I wasn't. I just Zoe, what's going on?

Zoe: I'm sorry. I shouldn't have I've got a lot on my mind.

Alia: Do you identify as Black?

Zoe: Yeah. Los dos.

Alia: And Rafa?

Zoe: Rafa says she's Latine and that's enough. Rafa has her own problems.

(Moment)

Alia: You seem pretty upset. Should I come back later?

Zoe: So any update on the show?

Alia: Oh yeah. I'm able to resubmit. Thank you for talking to—

Zoe: Of course. You're an incredible artist.

God, I wish there was a $5k award I could've submitted to in college.

Alia: Yeah. That's more than five months rent for me.

Zoe: I wish my rent was still nine hundred dollars.

Alia: I wish I was a world class artist.

Zoe: You are. The world is just always behind to realize it. I have something weird to ask you.

Alia: Weirder than asking about my genealogy .

Zoe: Yes. And sorry about that. I didn't mean to Can you not come over for dinner tonight?

Alia: Oh. Sure. Ximena and I already talked anyway and I really don't want to get back into it

Zoe: Wait she
Of course she did. She's always

ALIA: Is something happening with Ximena?

ZOE: Who else is in the art show? Do you have a list of names?

ALIA: I can pull them. Why?

ZOE: Were you the only artist Ximena had a problem with?

ALIA: Um, that I know of. I was the only one who was asked to pull my work.

ZOE: Yeah. Get me that list of names. Email it to me.

ALIA: Um okay.

Zoe, you don't work at the university. How are you going to I really don't want to make an issue of this.

ZOE: It's not an issue, Alia. I promise. I just need to

I don't want to cause problems for you either and I promise this won't. Okay?

ALIA: Okay.

(ALIA *sets the papers down and leaves the studio to get some air. Once she's outside,* ZOE *stabs the canvas.*)

Scene 8

(*Later that night, at home,* ZOE *drinks wine directly from the bottle at the dinner table. Dinner is not ready.* XIMENA *walks in. She's had a long day.*)

XIMENA: Oh. Hi.

ZOE: Hi.

XIMENA: Where's Alia?

ZOE: I asked her not to come.

XIMENA: Oh. Bad day? Did something happen?

ZOE: Kind of.

(*Moment.* XIMENA *hesitantly sits down.*)

XIMENA: If I'm about to get yelled at, I will say you did not send a warning shot this time.

ZOE: I was worried it would be a kill shot.

XIMENA: Honestly, Zoe, I am so sorry. I was frustrated that—

ZOE: Loren Davis.

(XIMENA *doesn't say anything.*)

ZOE: Do you know who that is?

XIMENA: Zoe.

ZOE: I'm assuming you're not planning on denying it?

XIMENA: I'm not sure that I

Zoe, could you start from the beginning?

ZOE: I think I just did.

XIMENA: It's complicated.

ZOE: No, it isn't.

XIMENA: What exactly did you hear?

ZOE: Ximena, are you serious right now? What did I hear?

XIMENA: I'm just wary that we might be having different conversations.

ZOE: How about this? You start the conversation you think we're having and then I'll let you know if we're having the same conversation.

(*Moment. A long moment*)

XIMENA: I love you. You know that right?

ZOE: Loren. Davis.

XIMENA: And there are lots of different pieces to this. It's not easy for me to just start talking.

ZOE: Is your name Loren Davis?

(*Moment*)

XIMENA: Yes.

ZOE: Where were you born?

XIMENA: Exactly where I told you. The Bronx.

ZOE: And the reason I haven't met your parents, the reason they weren't at the wedding, our fucking wedding is because they're   white?

XIMENA: Because they're homophobes. I haven't spoken to my parents since I was twenty. They kicked me out. Everything you know about me is true.

ZOE: Except your name.

XIMENA: You know how…shitty people can be. How if they think for even a second that you're appropriating a culture, you're canceled. No questions asked. I hated my parents. I wanted to change my name to reflect who I am.

ZOE: Your Cuban parents?

XIMENA: My mother, yes.

ZOE: And your father is white?

XIMENA: Yes.

ZOE: Why is this the first time we've talked about this? We've been together for ten years, Ximena.

XIMENA: I didn't think you'd
What I love about you is how open and accepting you are. I'm Cuban. Just because only one of my parents is Cuban that doesn't take that away from me. Campos is my mother's maiden name.

ZOE: And Ximena?

XIMENA: My grandmother's name. Zoe, I'm sorry. I didn't mean for this to be

It's a part of my past. There's a lot in my past I just don't like to talk about. My family is you. And Rafa. My birth family are dead to me. They've been dead to me since I left the house. And I've never looked back. I'm sorry. I know how hurtful this is. I didn't mean to be deceitful.

(*Moment*)

ZOE: What did you say to Alia?

XIMENA: I asked her to resubmit. And I apologized.

ZOE: You can't complain about gatekeeping and then be a gatekeeper.

XIMENA: I know. What I did was wrong. Thank you for calling me out on it. You sure you're okay? Are we okay?

ZOE: We're
I really gotta finish that commission. I should head to the studio.

XIMENA: Okay. Zoe, I am so sorry.

ZOE: Yeah, yeah. I know.

XIMENA: I should've told you years ago.

(ZOE *doesn't say anything. She just leaves.*)

Scene 9

(*The next afternoon.* RAFA *sits in her office. She's not even pretending to work this time. A moment before* ALIA *knocks on the door.*)

RAFA: Yeah. Come in.

ALIA: Is this a bad time?

RAFA: No this
I wasn't doing anything. What's up?

ALIA: I'm worried about Zoe.

RAFA: Oh?

ALIA: She slept in the studio last night. She's been asking me weird questions. And she just seems like she's spiraling.

RAFA: Weird questions?

ALIA: She asked me why I didn't identify as Afro-Latine when I've never said Anyway, I'm probably overthinking things but her last spiral was
I just didn't want to not say something.

RAFA: Has she been taking her medication?

ALIA: Yeah. She has. There's just something off. Usually, she says Ximena is her anchor but I think there may be something going on with them? And it's just
It felt safer to say something.

(Shift)

RAFA: Why'd you submit your work to a call that was for Latine artists if you don't identify as Afro-Latine or Latine at all?

ALIA: Rafa, I don't want to—

RAFA: I'm just trying to understand something.

ALIA: The call said art that represented and reflected Latinidad.

RAFA: Okay. So could a white person submit?

ALIA: No. But they listed countries out.

RAFA: And they listed Belize?

ALIA: What exactly are you trying to understand? I'm not here to defend I should go. I just wanted to give you a heads up about Zoe.

RAFA: I'm sorry. Please. Sit down.

(ALIA *hesitates.*)

RAFA: I used to be so mad my parents named me
Rafaela and named her Zoe. Growing up in LA in the
Nineties, going to private school, the last thing you
wanted to be was seen as a chola.
And Zoe. Zoe looks…Black. Everyone just thought she
was Black. And for a really long time, she let people
think that too.

ALIA: She is Black.

RAFA: And me? Apparently I look "Mexican." Black
Mexican is what they used to call me. They used to call
me wetback and asked if me I swam or jumped the
fence to get here.
Zoe separated herself from me. She was older and
cooler and said I needed to learn how to stick up
for myself. And that's why she distanced herself.
Eventually in high school, things changed. It was
cool to be Latina then. Then Zoe started speaking
Spanish and would wear her hair naturally instead
of straightening it all the time. I used to resent her for
that.

ALIA: For straightening her hair?

RAFA: For not being proud. Not until it was cool.
You need to understand that this isn't personal. I just
don't

ALIA: You don't get to just decide how
At least they called you Mexican. In Chicago, everyone
kept telling me "That's not Hispanic." Or "people from
Belize are just black" or "You're faking it to be cool."
And whenever I did speak Spanish, people made fun
of my accent. They called me negra, sucia,vaca. Every
single name you could think of. Some that I still can't
even repeat because they're too

It's one thing when white people bully you. It's a completely different thing when people from your own culture tell you aren't allowed in. I submitted my work, honestly, because I've always felt very connected to my Central American roots and wanted to show that. But I don't want to have to continue to defend my existence in Latinidad. It's draining. It feels like everyone wants to see my full DNA results before they listen to me when I tell them what I am.

RAFA: I'm sorry. I know I haven't always been—

ALIA: No one has. So that's why. That's why even though my dad is technically Mexican and my mom is Belizean, I say I'm Black. It's just easier than having to Having to do this every single time.

RAFA: I didn't know that about your dad.

ALIA: It shouldn't have mattered. I resent that I have to mention my barely Mexican father for people to hear me about my belonging. My mother is who taught me Spanish. My mother is who introduced me to our culture. And people disregard her so easily because some white people decided which part of Honduras belonged to Spain and which part to England. My mom's great-grandparents were Mayan but apparently that doesn't matter because Belize "doesn't count."

RAFA: That's not exactly how that happened. Belize has a more complex—

ALIA: We have been letting colonizers tell us who we are and that's not okay.

(*Moment*)

RAFA: Thank you again for the heads up about Zoe.

ALIA: Yeah. Of course.

RAFA: I have a right to be protective over my culture.

ALIA: Our culture, Rafa. (*She gets up to leave.*)

RAFA: Alia, I didn't mean—

ALIA: Rafa, I have class. I don't have time—

RAFA: I am truly thankful you stopped by to tell me about Zoe. I know what Zoe says about Ximena being her anchor but I've always joked her real wife is you. She spends more time with you than anyone else and I know her mood swings can be
It's nice to know there's someone else looking out for her.

ALIA: I've been obsessed with Zoe Castillo since I first saw her work the Denver Museum of Contemporary Art. She's a genius. I guess most geniuses have some extra pieces in their brains that sometimes malfunction.

RAFA: I guess so.

(ALIA *leaves.*)

Scene 10

(*The next evening.* RAFA *is at* ZOE *and* XIMENA*'s house.* RAFA *is pacing on the phone while* XIMENA *sits silently and still.*)

RAFA: Yes, please let me know the second you hear something. Yeah. Thanks. Bye. (*She hangs up the phone.*)

XIMENA: Anything?

(RAFA *shakes her head.*)

RAFA: I think she
She's fine. I'm sure of it.

XIMENA: It's been two days, Rafa.

RAFA: I know. Alia said something earlier to me too. She's been stressed about her commission. Maybe she's just working extra hours to get it done.

XIMENA: Her phone has been turned off.

RAFA: You know she hates having her phone on when she works. She's just I'm sure she's fine.

(*Moment*)

XIMENA: Were you the one who told her?

RAFA: What?

XIMENA: About Loren Davis.

RAFA: Ximena, listen, I don't want to be a part of this. Whatever is going on with your name isn't—

XIMENA: It's just that it's so much more complicated than you made it seem.

RAFA: I didn't make it seem like anything. I didn't even—

XIMENA: And now you've triggered an episode.

RAFA: Whoa. Wait. I didn't tell Zoe anything at all.

XIMENA: You're always causing so much trouble for us.

RAFA: Whoa. Ximena, you're not—

XIMENA: And now my wife is missing. I wish you would talk to me first but you always—

RAFA: Listen. It's not my fault that you lied to my sister for a decade about your real name and God knows what else. All I care about right now is making sure Zoe is okay. I didn't tell her about Loren Davis. And to be honest, I haven't asked any further questions because I don't have the mental capacity to deal with that bullshit right now. So you can back the fuck up.

XIMENA: I
I'm sorry. I'm just worried.

RAFA: Yeah.

(*The door opens and* ALIA *enters.*)

ALIA: She's in New York.

RAFA: What?

XIMENA: Why?

ALIA: I don't know. But she flew there last night.

RAFA: How do you know?

ALIA: She called me. From a random number.

RAFA: She's okay?

ALIA: She's okay.

XIMENA: What is she doing in New York?

ALIA: I don't know, Ximena. All I know is she said she's okay. Maybe she went to New York after talking to MASS MOCA?

RAFA: Was it on her schedule to go to—

ALIA: No but you know how Zoe is. And they've been pushing back the contract a ton so she probably just got frustrated and just flew there.

XIMENA: Did she say what part of New York?

ALIA: Brooklyn. Wait. Tribeca actually. I think. We really didn't talk that long.

RAFA: Thank God she's okay.

ALIA: She said she was sorry that she didn't mention it. She thought she could do the trip in a day.

RAFA: Of course she did. This is what happens when your sister is an artist.

XIMENA: And you don't know exactly where she is?

ALIA: Ximena, I was just she was okay.

RAFA: Did she say when she'd be back?

ALIA: Tomorrow night.

RAFA: Good. I'm going to head home. And then call my mother. Because I'm sure she's just as worried. (*She leaves.*)

ALIA: I should go too.

XIMENA: Was it you? Did you do this?

ALIA: Did I do what?

XIMENA: I will end your career for this.

ALIA: Ximena, I have no idea what you're talking about.

XIMENA: I will end your career for this.

(XIMENA *glares at* ALIA. ALIA *leaves*.)

Scene 11

(*The next afternoon.* ALIA *is in* ZOE'*s studio tidying up.* VALERY *enters.*)

VALERY: Oh hi.

ALIA: Hi.

VALERY: Is Zoe here?

ALIA: No she's out of town. Can I take a message? Are you a student at the university? She does gallery visits but by appointment only so I can—

VALERY: No. I mean, yes I'm a student but I We had talked before she left for When will she be back?

(*Moment*)

ALIA: Can I ask what you need from Zoe?

VALERY: It's kind of complicated.

ALIA: I haven't
Sorry to ask this but how do you know Zoe?

VALERY: We just met. A couple of days ago. And she was supposed to be
She called me two days ago trying to get some information and I just wanted to see what she found out.

ALIA: Some information?

VALERY: It's kind of personal.

ALIA: Is Zoe in some sort of [trouble]

VALERY: No, it's not
It's about her wife. Dr Campos.

ALIA: Oh. Well, Zoe should be back tonight. You can
tell her then.

VALERY: Do you know Dr—Ximena well?

ALIA: Not really. I took a class with her this semester
because Zoe suggested I I haven't had a lot of good
I don't know her. Not really.

VALERY: She's white.

ALIA: What?

VALERY: She's white. She's not Cuban.

ALIA: I don't
I don't understand.

VALERY: Yeah, crazy right? I can't even
At first I just had this feeling you know. Things came
up while we were working together one on one and
I was like "there's no way she's Cuban." But I didn't
think she was
But then I was like who would lie about being Cuban if
they were like Bolivian, you know? So I just kind of fell
into this research hole, trying to figure things out and
turns out she's white! Like full on white!

ALIA: I should get back to—

VALERY: I'm trying to get her outed to the university.
It's this whole thing. But yeah isn't that the biggest
mind fuck. She's white!

ALIA: Reported to the university for what?

VALERY: For lying about who she is.

ALIA: Will they care?

VALERY: Someone should!

(*Moment*)

ALIA: Did something else happen? Did she question your work or—

VALERY: Why does something else need to happen? She's been lying about who she is. She's been demoralizing and cruel all under the guise of pretending to be a Cuban woman.

ALIA: How do you know she's pretending?

VALERY: Because I just do! Or I had a feeling and then I followed through. But I've known the second I started working her one on one. And I have proof. I've had proof for a while and I don't know what we're waiting for.

(*Moment*)

ALIA: I'm Alia.

VALERY: Lia?

ALIA: Alia.

VALERY: Valery.

ALIA: I just realized we hadn't shared our names yet.

VALERY: Yeah. Hi.

ALIA: Who's we?

VALERY: What?

ALIA: You said "what we're waiting for." Who's we?

VALERY: Zoe, Rafa, and I.

(*Moment*)

VALERY: She's been stealing work from her students for years. Credited on major papers she's barely even proofread.
And I think I've finally got a really good idea for my thesis and I don't want

I cannot let my first major paper have a hypocrite
attached to it. And I don't want that to It would ruin
my
And the university really doesn't seem to care because
that's how the "mentorship" process works. And I just
This woman has been cosplaying in my culture for
decades and she could wreck my career before I even
really get a chance to
I just won't let that happen.
It's like when Rachel Dolezal—

ALIA: Yeah I
Ximena tried to get my work thrown out of a major
show because she said I wasn't—

VALERY: She's evil.

ALIA: I don't think she's evil. Deeply insecure maybe.

VALERY: You should see the way she talks to the Black
students.

ALIA: Don't do that.

VALERY: What?

ALIA: Try to connect with me by talking about Black
people.

VALERY: I wasn't trying to—

ALIA: You were. It's fine.

VALERY: She's just not very
I think anti-blackness is very deeply rooted for her.

ALIA: Her wife is Black.

VALERY: Zoe is Dominican.

ALIA: And Haitian.

VALERY: Haitian's aren't Black-Black.

(ALIA *sighs. Moment*)

VALERY: I sound awful. I'm not
I'm sorry. I'm not this person.

(ALIA *shrugs.*)

VALERY: I just, I see it. I see her anti-blackness and she claims it's part of her culture and she's not aware of her unconscious bias and it's just like fuck you for not only faking my culture but then adding a bad reputation to it. I'm not saying there isn't anti-blackness in Latinidad or even Cuban culture, I'm just saying fuck her for you know fanning a flame and like lighting a match and that didn't need to be lit or fanned or whatever the fuck she's doing.

ALIA: Very well-said.

VALERY: I don't think clearly when I'm angry.

ALIA: I see that.

VALERY: Have I totally put my foot in my mouth? Are you like Dominican or Puerto Rican or something?

ALIA: Why would you assume I'm not.

VALERY: I took this workshop. And it was all about unconscious bias. And I realized that I have a lot of my own shit that I need to process and work through and I'm trying to be better. But surely we can all admit that what Ximena is doing is wrong.

ALIA: I'm just having a hard time understanding. You believe Ximena is a white woman.

VALERY: Yes. Because she is.

ALIA: And you think this because?

VALERY: Because I talked to her brother Jimmy and Zoe went to see her family in New York.

ALIA: Ximena's? The super homophobic family?

VALERY: Yes.

(*Moment*)

ALIA: Why would she pretend to be Cuban?

VALERY: Because she's a sociopath.

ALIA: You have proof of this?

VALERY: Yes! Zoe probably does too.

ALIA: Wow. That means that she
(*She takes a minute to collect her thoughts. That means that
a white woman told her she wasn't Latine enough.*)

Scene 12

(RAFA *and* ZOE *are in her office.* RAFA *looks over pictures
and letters.*)

RAFA: Oh my God.

ZOE: Rafa, she's white! And not like "white Latina"
white. White-white. She's fucking white!

RAFA: I just
You met her parents?

ZOE: Yes! They loved me. They were so excited to
meet me finally and thought that I was—get this—
uncomfortable with them being Jewish! She told them I
was anti-Semitic.

RAFA: So wait. Ximena is Jewish?

ZOE: Loren Davis is.

RAFA: And her mother is—

ZOE: Polish! To give Ximena like ten percent of credit,
her mother was born in Cuba. But she's fucking Polish.
And identifies as Polish. Not Cuban.

RAFA: And her grandmother named Ximena?

ZOE: Oh! That's the best part. Her maid was named
Ximena. Ximena Campos.

RAFA: She named herself after her maid.

ZOE: La criada, Rafa!
I'm going to kill her.

(RAFA *pushes the papers away.*)

RAFA: Zoe, I know you're kidding Well I hope you're kidding You don't seem like

ZOE: Who's kidding? She's fucking white, Rafa!

RAFA: And that's infuriating for sure but murder?

ZOE: I have been married to someone who has been lying to me for a decade.

RAFA: So she's a sociopath. Divorce her. *(Moment)* Zoe, you're going to divorce her right? She's been lying to you.

ZOE: I haven't
I just didn't think I'd
Murder her? Sure. Divorce her?

RAFA: Is that hard for you to even consider divorce? Zoe, she's been lying to you for 10 years. How could you possibly—

ZOE: It's easier for me to hold onto the anger, Rafa.

RAFA: You can't possibly stay with her.

ZOE: She's my wife. I made a
Also, divorce? At my age? I'm not exactly a good sell. "Hi Tinder. Who wants to date a bipolar artist who even in her mid thirties still can't get her manic episodes under control?" Who's going to want to be with me? Who's going to [take care of me]

RAFA: Zoe, you cannot forgive this. Divorce isn't a death sentence. You can find someone who—

ZOE: Look how well divorce worked out for you.

(*Moment*)

ZOE: I'm sorry. I just
Divorce seems too major, Rafa. I'm not ready to be on
my own again. To deal with

RAFA: So you'd rather stay with someone you cannot
trust? Someone who values you so little that she—

ZOE: Please don't ask me to think about that right now.
I can't, Rafa.

(*A moment*)

RAFA: Isn't she one of the judges for that huge award
Alia is up for?

ZOE: Yes! Can you get her removed?

RAFA: That's not my department, Zoe.

ZOE: We have to do something.

RAFA: You can do something right now. I still have the
lawyer's number who handled my divorce.

ZOE: I don't want
I need some time, Rafa.

RAFA: Zoe, you can't honestly—

ZOE: I know! I know. I just
All of this doesn't mean I'm not still madly in love with
Ximena Campos.

RAFA: Ximena Campos doesn't exist.

(*Moment*)

ZOE: How did I not see it? I should've seen it. I
should've heard it in her Spanish. In the way she
talked about
Was I just that desperate for love?
But it's not just me. She's fooled everyone. She's a
major activist. She's published. People across the
country look up to her.
Do you think maybe it's just a [misunderstanding]
Some of the stuff she knew was just too specific.

RAFA: She's been studying our culture for a long time. Turns out you can get specific.

(ZOE *looks at the picture of Loren.*)

ZOE: I love her, Rafa.

RAFA: You don't know her, Zoe.

(ZOE *sets the picture down before picking it up again and ripping it.*)

Scene 13

(*In their living room,* ZOE *sits down drinking coffee and reading a book. She's not really reading.* XIMENA *walks in and* ZOE *immediately throws the book at her.*)

XIMENA: Zoe?

ZOE: You fucking lied!

XIMENA: Lied? Zoe, what are you
I didn't lie. My parents are—

ZOE: Your parents are great! They were excited to meet me. And to learn, fun fact, that I do not hate Jewish people.

XIMENA: Zoe.

ZOE: Do not fucking start with me, Xime—Loren. Do not fucking start with me.

(*A moment. It's tense.* ZOE *takes a breath.*)

ZOE: And the Bronx? Jesus, Ximena. Is everything you told me a lie?

XIMENA: I told you it was complicated. When I was with Ximena, we would go to the Bronx. I spent more time there than—

(ZOE *throws something else in* XIMENA's *direction. She then pulls out a stack of letters.*)

XIMENA: Zoe, I don't want to talk about my parents. I
don't even really know—

ZOE: You wrote them every week.

XIMENA: I
Zoe, how do you even know that the people you met
my parents? They could've been—

ZOE: Strangers who have your letters. Loren?
Seriously?

XIMENA: How did you even find them? We aren't—

ZOE: Jimmy. Which another lie because you told me
you were an only child. Jimmy and I are Facebook
friends now. We're real close. He was so surprised
to learn that his baby sister had gotten married and
wanted to know if he could send a wedding gift.
Should I send him our address?
Speak up, Loren. Now isn't the time to—

XIMENA: Don't dead name me.

ZOE: Oh my fucking God. You are disgusting. I can't
believe you
I know nothing about you. Nothing! Ten years, Loren.
And everything I thought I knew turned out to be a lie.

(Shift)

ZOE: Our marriage Our life
It's all bullshit.
Thank God we never had children because that would
just be—

XIMENA: Zoe, I'm still me.

ZOE: I don't know who that is. The "still me" who
visited Cuba every summer? Because that's bullshit.
The "still me" who named themselves after their
grandmother? Because that's bullshit. The "still me"
who wants their ashes to be taken back to Havana?
Because that's bullshit.

XIMENA: You're not giving me a chance to exp lain.

ZOE: You know what your mother told me? She told me when you were a kid, you pretended to be Puerto Rican. How many cultures have you stolen, Loren? God, were you ever Korean?

XIMENA: Zoe.

ZOE: No. Of course not. So you stuck with Latinidad. What was I? Just a way to confirm that you really were who you said you were.

XIMENA: I love you, Zoe.

ZOE: How could you honestly believe that?

XIMENA: Please. Zoe, please.
Just give me a chance to explain.

(A moment. Another really tough moment.)

XIMENA: The core of who I am is the same.

ZOE: I have no idea what that means, Xi—Loren. What is the core—

XIMENA: I still believe in all the same things.

ZOE: You stole my culture.

XIMENA: My maid raised me more than my parents ever did.

ZOE: Holy shit.

XIMENA: I just
What are kids like me supposed to do? I grew up around an all Latine community.

ZOE: No you didn't.

XIMENA: Yes I did. Like I said, I spent way more time in the Bronx than I did in Tribeca. I grew up speaking Spanish. This culture is mine.

ZOE: That's not how it works.

XIMENA: My mother was born in Cuba.

ZOE: If I was born in China, that doesn't make me Chinese.

XIMENA: It kind of does.

ZOE: No it doesn't

XIMENA: Only because race is bullshit. It's not based on a real thing. This culture is mine, Zoe. I didn't fake anything. I did this to uplift the culture. Look how much attention my work has gotten our community. I did it for us. For mi gente.
Am I supposed to throw all of that away just because technically my parents, who I have no real relationship with are Jewish? Yes. I wrote them letters but read them. They're short and lack details.
If you had talked to Ximena, you'd know who my real mother is.
I don't regret what I've done. I regret the way I've done it though. I should've never lied to you, Zoe.
I just
To me it wasn't lying.

(Moment)

ZOE: It was bad enough that you were a sociopath. But Jesus, now you're a sociopath and a victim. I guess that's how I should've known. White women are always so quick to play victim. You can't steal your maid's culture, Loren and then make yourself some sort of martyr. That's not how it works. *(She tosses papers down on the table.)*

XIMENA: Don't do this, Zoe. We can fix this. I love—

ZOE: I want a divorce. And I'm calling Valery, that student of yours. And confirming everything on Monday. So you know, enjoy the art show, be a judge, do what you have to, but come Monday it all comes crashing the fuck down. *(She leaves the house and slams the door behind her.)*

Scene 14

(Much later that night, ALIA walks around the studio holding a switch blade. There's glass everywhere and the art work ZOE had been working on is completely destroyed. It looks like someone broke in.)

ALIA: Hello! I have a knife. I don't really want to call the cops in case you're a person of color but I will.

(Moment. ALIA keeps looking around. ZOE walks into the general area holding a bottle of wine, looking absolutely dishelveled.)

ZOE: Alia?

ALIA: Zoe, what're you
I thought someone broke in.

ZOE: Someone did. Me.

ALIA: You broke the glass?

ZOE: I left my key at my house and I just What're you doing here, Alia?

ALIA: I was getting a drink with a friend at the bar down the street and parked behind the studio. When I saw the broken glass, I thought
Zoe, are you okay?

ZOE: No, I'm not. *(She drinks from the bottle.)*

ALIA: I'm going to call Rafa. *(She pulls out her phone.)*

ZOE: No, wait. Please don't. I don't want
I just need some time.

ALIA: Zoe, this is bad.

ZOE: I know. I
It's funny. Right after I broke the glass, I left an email for the glass repair guy . At least even in a breakdown, I'm resourceful.

ALIA: Yeah.

(Moment)

ALIA: Zoe, what's going on?

ZOE: Oh you know, my marriage is falling apart. I'm not anywhere near close to getting this commission done because as soon as I deal with one exp losion in my personal life, there's immediately another one.

ALIA: So it's true? About Ximena?

ZOE: It's fucking true.

ALIA: Zoe, si necesitas algo—

ZOE: Necesito una otra vida.
Wait you never speak in Spanish.

ALIA: I was trying to let you know how serious I was.

(ZOE nods and sets the bottle of wine down.)

ZOE: Why
Why do you never speak in Spanish?

ALIA: Growing up kids would tease me so I got in my head about it. Zoe, please let me call for help.

ZOE: In a second. So that's it? Some kids teased you and you tossed away your culture?

ALIA: My culture? I didn't realize
I don't think you understand how brutal kids, and honestly adults too, can be.

ZOE: Yes I do.

ALIA: I am so sorry about Ximena.

ZOE: Me too.

(ALIA and ZOE are in silence for a bit. ALIA looks around to see the mess. ZOE kind of wavers back and forth.)

ZOE: It makes so much sense on paper right? Like the right thing to do is leave my wife and never look back. But, I built a life with this person. And it was just
How I recover from something like this?

ALIA: I don't know. But you're not alone.

ZOE: I feel like a piece of me has been ripped out and can never ever be replaced. Like for the rest of my life I'll be incomplete. I'm incomplete.

ALIA: You're hurting. But you're not incomplete. You're just…my mom used to say that our heart don't break; they just reconstruct. After each loss, we have to rebuild. You're not broken. You're not incomplete. You're just under reconstruction.

ZOE: I can't go back there. I can't—

ALIA: You don't have to. I'm sure Rafa would let you stay in the extra bedroom for a bit.

ZOE: But all of my stuff is

ALIA: Rafa and I can get it for you. You never have to see Ximena ever again if you don't want to.

ZOE: That's not true.

ALIA: You're right. It's not. But I will do everything I can to make each meeting with her as short as possible. Zoe, you're not going through this alone. We're here. Both Rafa and I. Would it be okay if I called

ZOE: Yeah. Thank you. Yeah, call Rafa. You'll give me a ride?

ALIA: Of course.

(ZOE *nods and takes in her studio, the damage surrounding her.* ALIA *notices as she dialing.*)

ALIA: You're not alone, Zoe. I mean it. [on the phone] Hi Rafa. It's Alia.

(ALIA *steps away to finish the call.* ZOE *picks up a piece of paper and pencil and begins a new approach to the commission, attempting to create amidst the chaos.*)

Scene 15

(Two days later. The day of the art show contest for ALIA. ALIA *is pacing around in a gallery. She's excited.* VALERY, RAFA, *and* XIMENA *are there.* VALERY *sees* ALIA. *[In a staged production they would be wearing masks as they're indoors in 2020.])*

VALERY: Congrats on being a finalist.

ALIA: Thank you. I'm so excited I'm shaking.

VALERY: I can see that.
They decide soon, right?

ALIA: Yeah. Super soon. I will cry if I don't win. I think I'll cry if I do win.

VALERY: Is that Loren Davis over there?

ALIA: It is. You gonna cover her in pig's blood?

VALERY: Pig's blood?

ALIA: I was thinking a mix of Bay of Pigs and that movie Carrie.

*(*VALERY *shrugs.* ALIA *realizes her misstep.)*

VALERY: Have you heard from Zoe?

ALIA: She'll be around later. Maybe.

VALERY: Oh. I was hoping she'd—

ALIA: She sometimes needs extra time to recharge.

VALERY: Yeah.

*(*XIMENA *starts to use a knife to clink her glass.)*

XIMENA: Ladies and gentleman! We're so glad you're all here. We're here to celebrate some amazing Latine and Latinx artists who are truly put their blood, sweat, and tears into their work. But first, there's something I need to come clean about.
It is my duty to inform you I have stepped down from my position here at the university. I have been

dishonest and my behavior has been rooted in anti-blackness and only furthers violence against the Black and Latine/x community.

My name is Loren Davis. I grew up in New York with my mother and father, who are both Jewish.

My parents were incredibly distant and I was raised by the Latinx community around me. I realize now the violence of my actions and would like to take this time to apologize, publicly, to all of you.

(ZOE *enters.* XIMENA *notices.*)

XIMENA: I thought what I was doing was for us.

(ZOE *glares at* XIMENA. XIMENA *continues her speech.*)

XIMENA: For our shared community but after an evening of reflection surrounded by art that celebrates and ignites Latinidad, I feel called to be open about who I am.

I would also like to take this time to apologize to Alia Smith, who, in my attempt to preserve Latinidad, I use anti-black tactics by questioning her belonging in this sacred place. Alia, I hope that through time you and I can mend what I've broken between us.

While I'm stepping down here at the university, I still feel my work is incredibly important and my hope is professors here still feel comfortable using them as a resource.

This controversy is specific to my identity and not to my research which has helped thousands. Moving forward, I will continue my research but this time under the blended name of Loren Campos because I truly do feel I have lived and continue to live a blended identity.

It is my honor to congratulate the finalist, Marisa Ochoa, Alia Smith, and Rebecca Ramos. You all have created such great works of art and have added to a long legacy of proud Latin art. The winner tonight of the cash prize is Rebecca Ramos.

(XIMENA *pauses for applause. No one does.*)

VALERY: What the fuck.

XIMENA: Let us join in applause to celebrate Rebecca Ramos. I realize the news of my stepping down is heavy but let us not forget why we're here.

(RAFA *eventually begins to clap. Other join.* ZOE *and* VALERY *do not clap.*)

XIMENA: Rebecca, you are a guiding light. I know you may not want to right now but I'm happy to make myself available to you should you want further criticism and praise on your wonderful work of art. Thank you everyone.

(XIMENA *makes a step towards* ZOE. *Both* RAFA *and* ALIA *step forward to stop her.* XIMENA *leaves.*)

VALERY: What. The. Fuck.

Scene 16

(*That evening. Outside in a parking lot,* VALERY, ALIA, ZOE, *and* RAFA *all sit on the sidewalk corner, drinking. They're each drinking out their own personal mini wine boxes.*)

VALERY: Did that just happen?

ZOE: Yes.

VALERY: Did she really step down?

RAFA: I got the email about twenty minutes ago. She's no longer a tenured professor but they're still asking her to be a lecturer.

VALERY: Seriously? *(She pulls out her phone to check her email.)* Dean Vilas wants to see first thing Monday morning to discuss a new co-author for my paper.

RAFA: Congrats.

VALERY: I didn't want
I mean yes, thank you.
I wanted to get someone who I didn't want it like this.

ZOE: This was the only way it was going to happen.

VALERY: Zoe, I'm sorry. I didn't want—

ZOE: It's fine. We wanted the truth and we got it. *(Moment. To* ALIA*)* Are you okay?

ALIA: No.

ZOE: I should've noticed how cruel she [was to you]

ALIA: It's not on you to apologize for her. I just
I think I'm still processing all of it. Holy shit, you know?
A white woman cosplaying as a Latina told me I wasn't Latina enough. Like that's all that there is to say.

VALERY: I didn't realize you were

ALIA: Please don't finish that sentence.

VALERY: Sorry.

ALIA: I'm just dumbstruck. I thought I was okay but
That there were bigger things to be upset about but
But hearing that speech just triggered everything all over again.
I've been fighting for people to see me as Latina, Latine, whatever, my whole life. I have been defending why I speak Spanish, that I don't just conveniently have a "good accent." I have dealt with nonstop questioning and exclusion and all this white woman had to do was dye her hair. A white woman decided which of us got five thousand dollars. A white woman made a profit at the expense of people like me for,

what two decades before she was called? What is there left to say?

VALERY: I just feel like we're protective of our culture because everyone is so willing to try it on. We don't mean to be—

ALIA: And yet I was left out and white woman made millions. Got a university job that some Afro-Latina probably applied for. She stood in a space, easily, that I haven't even been given the directions to.

(Moment)

RAFA: I know this is the wrong moment to say this but the timing of her speech was super fucked right?

ZOE: Yes.

I told her I was going to talk to Valery and tell the university on Monday. So I guess she felt she needed to do something first.

RAFA: You confronted her?

ZOE: I did.

(Moment)

RAFA: *(To* ALIA*)* I'm sorry.

VALERY: Me too.

ALIA: It's fine.

RAFA: It's not. You're right. You're trying to just get into the room and instead we let a white woman own the building.

ALIA: There's a reason this keeps happening.

RAFA: I know.

VALERY: I really didn't mean—

ALIA: Let's not all have an apology circle jerk. It's fine. The person we're all mad at right now is Ximena— What is it now? Loren Campos.

ZOE: I should've killed her.

ALIA: Yeah. We should've.

ZOE: I don't think I'd look cute in a jumpsuit.

RAFA: There are other bigger problems.

ZOE: No. Aesthetics are everything for artists.

(Moment)

VALERY: Am I going to have to do a full background search on every professor who claims to be Latinx/e? Like is this just where we're at now?

ALIA: Not just the professors. Rebecca Ramos isn't Latine either.

RAFA: She's Filipina right? I cross-checked that list you and Zoe sent. And yeah she's—

ZOE: I guess she has Spanish blood. Gross. Now there I go talking about bloodlines. This is all just too fucking messy.

(They all nod.)

ZOE: Is Ximen--Loren right? Is race just bullshit? Should we all just say fuck it and pick up whatever culture we want that day because none of makes any sense and the lines aren't clear and all this gatekeeping is destroying our community.

ALIA: I don't know about the rest of that but I think we can all agree that Loren, whatever her real last name is, is not right.

VALERY: Yeah fuck her.

(Moment)

RAFA: I have some books of hers in my office we can burn. I've always liked setting things on fire. It's therapeutic.

ZOE: I need to head the studio. I'm fucked. I need to have something to turn in by next week. Have fun burning her stuff. *(She gets up.)*

RAFA: We're going to be okay, Zoe.

ZOE: Yeah, I know.

ALIA: We're okay.
Also, Loren Campos doesn't get to define what's bullshit and what isn't. Only we can do that. I'm not saying there's not a lot of bullshit in Latinidad. But it's our bullshit.

(A moment)

ZOE: It's our bullshit.

ALIA: She will never know what it's like to wake at 6 am on Saturday to smell of the purple Faboloso and loud rancheras.

VALERY: Rancheras? In Belize?

ZOE: It's more common than you think.

(ALIA, recognizing that from saying she said earlier to Zoe, smiles. ZOE smiles back. A moment of understanding and being seen between the two of them.)

RAFA: A limpiar! / Vamo a limpiar

ZOE: Ay. Or burning your hands flying to flip the tortillas with your hands.

VALERY: Or stealing croquetas while abuelita sings her boleros.

ALIA: Dancing barefoot in the kitchen to Selena.

VALERY: Ay! Selena? You mean Celia Cruz.

ALIA: I said what I said.

(The women laugh together.)

RAFA: *(Singing dramatically)*
Ay, no hay que llorar

(No hay que llorar)
Que la vida es un carnaval
Que es más bello vivir cantando

(Music begins to play. Something like It's La vida es un carnaval by Celia Cruz. They're all gonna be okay.)

(And fuck Loren Davis. And Jessica Krug. And Rachel Dolezal. And Hillary Baldwin. They'll never have what we have.)

END OF PLAY

www.ingramcontent.com/pod-product-compliance
Lightning Source LLC
Chambersburg PA
CBHW061720130726
47996CB00006B/2409